This book
Gift

from

---

to

---

date

Your Marriage and Your Ancestry

a deliverance manual for
Singles and Married

DR D. K. OLUKOYA

YOUR MARRIAGE AND YOUR ANCESTRY
a deliverance manual for Singles and Married
(c) 2012 Dr. D. K Olukoya

ISBN: 978-978-920-019-1

December, 2012

A Publication of
Mountain of Fire and Miracles Ministries
International Headquarters, Lagos Nigeria.

All rights reserved. No portion of this book may be reproduced, stored in a retrieval system, or transmitted into any form or by any means electronic, mechanical, photocopy, recording, or any other except for brief quotations in printed review, without the prior written permission of the publisher.

All scripture quotations are from the King James Version of the Bible, unless otherwise stated.

Contents

Preface
7

Chapter One:
A CALL TO FIGHT TO FINISH
11

Chapter Two:
THE MYSTERY OF YOUR ANCESTRY
25

Chapter Three:
CAPTIVES OF THE TERRIBLE
45

Chapter Four:
SPIRITUAL DIAGNOSIS
59

Chapter Five:
STEPS TO FREEDOM
93

Preface

Rev.12:7-9:

> 'And there was war in heaven: <u>Michael and his angels fought</u> against the dragon; <u>and the dragon fought</u> and his angels and prevailed not; neither was their place found any more in heaven. And the great dragon was cast out, that old serpent, called the Devil, and Satan, which deceived the whole world: he was cast out into the earth, and his angels were cast out with him'.

When did fighting and warfare begin? What is the origin of warfare? Spiritual warfare actually started from heaven when Angel Michael fought and threw Lucifer out of heaven and there was chaos. If heaven have to fight, to bring the promises of God to pass, you must not find it strange that you have war to fight over your marriage. And immediately Lucifer was thrown out of heaven, there was peace. Hence, the battle of your life is not abnormal but the beautiful thing I must remind you about is that you have the authority to declare war and attain peace. Your prayer may not be wise if you say there should be no more battle; there will always be, yet our victory is sure in Jesus! Therefore, your ultimate task should now be to throw away 'Lucifer' from the tabernacle of your life so that there can be peace. If you throw him out once, he will constantly make attempts to come back, so no further chance or door should be left for his accessibility. More so, the current challenges you are going through may just be a tree of your faith. Beloved, all you need to do is never give the devil a legal hold over your life. If angels have to fight to enforce the purpose of God on earth, since our Father is a man of war, we His children cannot be civilians.

I want you to take the following prayer points, as you get ready for the deep revelation in this powerful book.

1. Strange voice speaking against my marital life, shut up now, in the name of Jesus.

2. My divine wife/husband, wherever you are, hear the word of the Lord, manifest and locate me, in the name of Jesus.

3. Power hiding my divine husband/wife, die, in the name of Jesus.

4. Any power that has declared that my wedding bell shall not ring, expire, in the name of Jesus.

5. Every domestic witchcraft behind my marital delays, receive divine judgment now and die, in the name of Jesus.

6. Household witchcraft behind my marital problem/delay, receive the stones of fire and set me free, in the name of Jesus.

7. Today, I declare that every mouth that ever mocked me, shall turn around to congratulate me, in the name of Jesus.

8. I decree, that anyone who has ever belittled me shall become little from today, because I shall go up higher, in the might name of Jesus.

9. Any evil bird, flying against my marriage shall fall down and die, in the mighty name of Jesus.

10. Every Goliath boasting against my marital breakthrough, fall down and die, in the name of Jesus.

11. Every anti-marriage curse, speaking against my marital life, be broken by the blood of Jesus, in the name of Jesus.

12. Every pattern of marital frustration in my family tree, clear away from my destiny, in the name of Jesus.

13. Every power speaking confusion and cloudiness, against my marital breakthrough, scatter, in the name of Jesus.

14. Anti-marriage yokes, anti-marriage bondage, anti-marriage chains, anti-marriage fetters, break, in the name of Jesus.

CHAPTER ONE

A Call To Fight To Finish

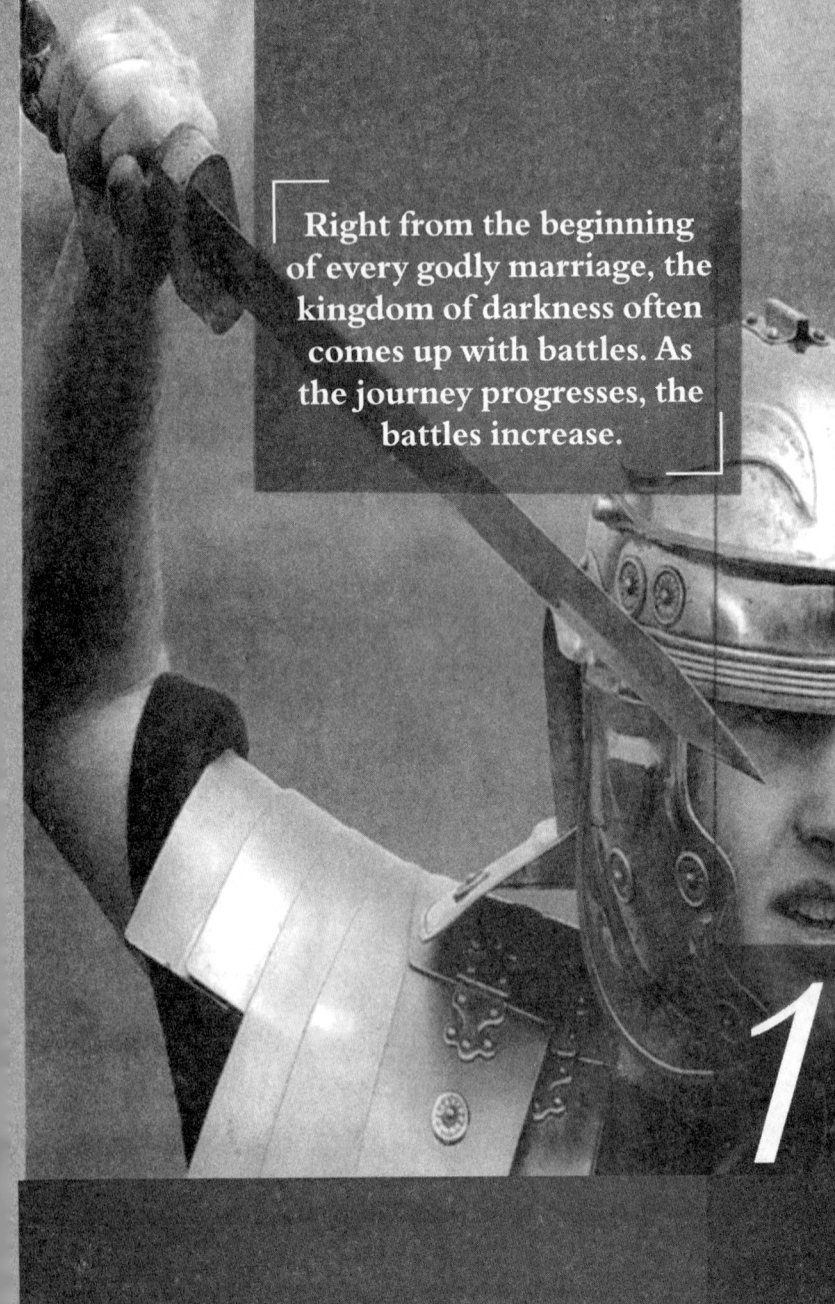

Right from the beginning of every godly marriage, the kingdom of darkness often comes up with battles. As the journey progresses, the battles increase.

1

■ CHAPTER ONE

A Call To Fight To Finish

Life is a battle. There is no realm where the battles of life are more pronounced than the realm of marriage. Marriage is not a joke. You can succeed in other areas of life with ease. But you need a great deal of effort to succeed on the field of marriage. Negligence is costly when it comes to the area of marriage. It is indeed true that as you lay your bed, so you will lie on it. Failure to put a solid foundation in place will jeopardise the building called marriage.

The kind of marriage you choose is the kind of marriage you will get. Your attitude to marriage will affect the kind of marriage you will get. When you seriously and painstakingly erect a solid foundation for your future in the area of marriage, you will reap huge dividends in the years ahead. Therefore, you need to take cognisance of the fact that the effort you put into preparations for your marriage, will eventually pay off. On the other hand, carelessness or negligence will also yield their fruits accordingly. I earnestly plead with you to meticulously take note of the entire contents of this book. What you are going to read from cover to cover, will have a position impact on your now and in the future. Of all area of life, marriage is not an area where you cannot afford to play games.

> *When you pursue the goals of marriage sincerely and vigorously, you will enjoy the benefits as long as you live.*

I have a serious burden for those who are undertaking the crucial journey to the realm of marriage. This journey is not the type that you can embark on with your eyes closed and your mouth shut. Those who have decided to be deaf and blind have fallen into the ditch of marital accidents. The watchword is: **watch! Be alert and avoid careless mistakes.** Those who neglected the hunter's whistle have been devoured by the wolves that beseech the field of marriage. Good preparation, keen watchfulness and giving meticulous attention to divine instructions, will save you from becoming one of the preys of the terrible power that have destroyed several homes today. No matter how tough a situation is, you will survive the topsy-turvy conditions of marriage. The moment you combine your personal effort with divine resource, which are already made available to you, you will discover that your marriage will become a source of pleasure and joy rather than a source of pain and regret.

SERIOUS CHALLENGES ♦♦♦

The challenges of marriage, though numerous, can be handled when you invite God into the journey of your marriage. There is nothing God cannot handle. There is no situation in the realm of marriage that is ever beyond the strength and wisdom of the Almighty.

> *Once you align yourself with God, you form an unbeatable team. The battle of marriage will be fought and won.*

The grey areas will be handled effectively through divine wisdom. God will make your home; heaven on earth. You shall not record failure or casualty. God will be there for you when you need help and divine intervention. You will receive the blueprint that will make your marriage the brightest and the best.

Take note of this, beloved, you must be prepared to put in place the necessary ingredients that will ensure a successful marriage. However, the first step that you ought to take, is to begin with preparations in the area of prayer. The arena of marriage has been bombarded with repeated battles. Right from the beginning of every godly marriage, the kingdom of darkness often come up with battles. As the journey progresses, battles increase. Knowing God's will is filled with battle because the devil determines to induce failure instead.

Obtaining parental consent, in some cases, is a battle. There are battles during courtship period. Battles are fought even on the day of the wedding. By the time the couple settles down and begins to establish a new family, there will be lots of battles to contend with. The period of child-bearing and child training are times of intense battles too. To raise children from their infant years till they grow up as adults, you will need to fight some battles. It does not make any sense whatsoever for anyone to undertake the journey into marriage, without being prepared to give what it takes in order to win the battle entailed thereof. As far as God is concerned, you are destined to have a smooth and a successful marriage. However, this can only be achieved when you pray your way through the various milestones of those great journey.

> *The more prayer efforts you put into your marital plans, the more you will succeed at reaching the peak of marital bliss.*

Even if you assume that there are no problems on the way, you should still pray.

THE WEAPON OF PRAYER ♦♦♦

You cannot pray enough when it comes to the issue of marriage. The more you pray, the greater your chance of achieving a glorious marriage. Prayer gives you the opportunity to draw upon divine resources. Prayer will enable you to bring out the best in and obtain the best from your partner. Prayer will establish your marriage and settle your future home. Prayer will cancel anti-marriage curses. It will remove the cobwebs of darkness from every part of your home. Sincere praying will save you from errors as far as the choice of partner is concerned. Prayer will prepare you to be your best as you plan for and work towards establishing a godly family.

Prayer will prepare your heart to receive divine directions. Prayer will safeguard your steps and grant you wisdom as you undertake steps to actualise your dreams.

Prayer will open the treasure of financial resources for your home. Prayer will silence every opposition that is being put in place by the power of your father's house. Prayer will give you peace and assurance. Prayer will shut the mouth of lions and convert the enemies in the area of marriage, to toothless dogs that can neither back nor bite. Prayer will grant you angelic assistance and magnetise your helpers. Prayer will imbue you with patience and other necessary virtues in the area of marriage, and make your home too hot for the enemy to handle. Prayer will make the spiritually blind to see and the spiritually deaf to hear. Prayer will sweep away the debris of confusion.

Prayer will grant you access to prophetic instructions. It will also enable you speak the right words in due season. Prayer will anchor you to divine sufficiency. When you address the journey of marriage at the altar of prayer, the occasional hiccups will disappear. If you want your marriage to beat the best and be the best, try prayers today. God is waiting for you at the altars of prayer. There are certain revelations you cannot receive, until you begin to pray. There are certain battles you cannot win until you make use of the artillery of prayer. As far as marriage is concerned, prayer is the master key. When you pray, the unavailable partner shall become available. Even if you feel that you are too old to get married or whether your marriage has gone too far for some necessary remedy, God will press the fast-forward button for your sake. You will not only get married with speed, the benefits shall be delivered to you miraculously. Herein lies the secrets of a glorious marriage.

> *Prayer is the only force in the universe that can add value to your marriage.*

When you pray, even those around you will find it difficult to understand the secrets behind your uncommon success. No wonder the Bible says:

Luke 18:1

> *And he spoke a parable unto them to this end, that men ought always to pray, and not to faint;*

enemy understands is the language of violence. You must fight for your freedom. The Bible says:

Genesis 27:40

> *And by the sword shalt thou live, and shalt serve thy brother; and it shall come to pass when thou shalt have the dominion that thou shalt break his yoke from off neck.*

In breaking the satanic yokes attached to your marriage, it goes beyond making positive confessions; it has to involve an 'enough is enough' readiness in the place of prayer. Even if you are an expert in phonetics and Queen's English, anti-marriage yokes cannot be broken until you have dominion. Let me tell you this secret, beloved, the spiritual realm rules the physical.

> *When you break through obstacle in your marriage in the spiritual realm, you shall experience ease and freedom In the physical realm.*

Herein lies one of the deep ordinances of heaven. The dominion you obtain in the spiritual realm, will be the amount of dominion which you will enforce on earth.

SPIRITUAL ORDINANCES ♦♦♦

I want you to read the passage below repeatedly.

Job 38:33

> *Knowest thou ordinances of heaven? Canst thou set the dominion thereof in the earth?*

When you know the ordinances of heaven, you will achieve uncommon dominion in your marital journey. When you grasp the truth of heavenly ordinances, no power from the kingdom of darkness will be able to mess up with your marriage. You need to pray and give the devil a shock treatment. What is the best way of handling battle in the area of marriage? Let us go back to the beginning.

Revelation 12:7-9

> *And there was war in heaven: Michael and his angels fought against the dragon; and the dragon fought and his angels, and prevailed not; neither was their place found any more in heaven. And the great dragon was cast out, that old serpent, called the Devil, and Satan., which deceiveth the whole world; he was cast out into the earth, and his angels were cast out into the earth, cast out with him.*

Just as there was war in heaven, there is war along the pathway of anyone traveling on the highway of marriage today. The only response that will save the day, is to face the devil squarely and tackle him weapon for weapon and fire for fire. Heaven's response to satanic rebellion or revolt is that satan was fought to a standstill and cast out. The only way you can win the battle against your marriage, is to fight. When Lucifer was thrown out of heaven, there was peace. Beloved, whatever has to be thrown out of your life in order to enable you achieve peace and success in your marriage, shall be thrown out by fire, in the name of Jesus. When you begin the battle of marriage, you must not be tempted to stop halfway. You must fight until victory is won.

CHAPTER TWO

The Mystery of your Ancestry

There is more to this than meets the eyes when a man who comes from his own background decides to be joined in wedlock with a lady, who comes from another background.

CHAPTER TWO

The Mystery of Your Ancestry

You may ask, why should anyone think of fighting battles in the area of marriage? Is there anything spiritual about marriage? Is marriage not a mere union between a man and a woman? Good question! Marriage is more than a union. There is more to this than meets the eyes when a man who comes from his own background, decides to be joined in wedlock with a lady, who comes from another background. Let me tell you this, beloved, no man or woman is an island. No matter how educated, enlightened or connected you are, you are a product of your ancestors. Even if you reside in the most developed part of the world, there is an invisible thread that binds you to your ancestors. unless you go into serious spiritual warfare sessions, your ancestry can hinder or affect your marriage negatively.

Beloved, your marriage rises or falls on your ancestry. Unknown to many people, the extent they will go in the area of marriage has been predetermined by their ancestors. Many young men and women today are merely swimming against an evil tide. Many have made several marriage proposals and failed at each attempts, the results will be repeated failure. Until the problem of ancestral marital embargo is tackled, many will continue to go in circles, without achieving anything. The solution is to examine the foundation and tackle marital problems from the role in your marriage. Hence, you cannot afford to dismiss your foundation with a wave of the hand. One of the deepest truths that can be found in the Bible is embedded in the passage below.

Ezekiel 16:4-6

> *And as for thy nativity, in the day thou wast born thy navel was not cut, neither wast thou washed in water to supple thee; thou wast not salted at all, nor swaddled*

at all . None eye pitied thee, to do any of these unto thee, to have compassion upon thee; but thou wast cast out in the open field, to the lothing of thy person, in the day that thou wast born. And when I passed by thee, and saw thee polluted in thine own blood, I said unto thee when thou wast in thy blood, Live; yea, I said unto thee when thou wast in thy blood, Live.

YOUR NATIVITY ◆◆◆

The depth of this truth is yet to be understood by modern man. Until this mystery is unraveled, you cannot understand why many are facing difficulties in the area of marriage. Here, the word nativity is used in the scripture to refer to your place of birth, origin or ancestry. Simply put, it refers to the umbilical cord, a biological part of the body by which a baby receives nourishment while in the womb. No matter what you have achieved today, there was a day when you came to this world as a helpless infant. Though your navel, which today, has been separated from your umbilical cord may be seen as an ordinary part of the body. It should actually remind you that it was formerly the rope that tied you to your parents and by extension, your ancestors who lived hundreds of years ago. This is a deep spiritual understanding you must not ignore. Just as there is no human being without a navel, there is no man or a woman who was not formerly linked to his or her parents through the umbilical cord.

The mystery of the umbilical cord or the placenta is so deep that it covers every area of life including marriage. No doubt, you are reading this book as an adult and your ancestors who died several years ago may not even be known by you, yet a powerful spiritual blood, once flew between you and your forebears or ancestors. Much as you want to live your own life, you cannot lay claim to the fact that your ancestry has no impact on your present life. Ignorance of this fact will continue to lead to marital delay, disappointments, courtship breakups, infertility, jilt and even divorce.

> *Until you address your marital roots, you have not yet taken the first step towards marriage, even if you are married.*

This is the major battle you must fight; the battle to be cut off from your root.

THE EVIL CURRENT ♦♦♦

When you overcome at this threshold, the journey of marriage will become so easy that you will wonder why people complain about marital problems. Beloved, when you were in the womb and your navel was not cut or served from the umbilical cord or the placenta, a lot of things were passing from your mother to you; these things may continue to trouble you later in life. Your mother who gave birth to you is an official representatives of your ancestors. Unknown to many people, negative currents that were loaded with curse, evil covenants, bondage and evil mechanism; some of these were sown into your life as an evil seed. Portions of the ancestral inflow were conveyed into your life in form of a time bomb waiting for explosion. The only way you can tell me that you are not going to pray against marital problems in the area of marriage is if you came into the world without umbilical cord. Beloved, I am sure you did not drop from the sky.

It is quite easy to say that you are living your own life. But, the moment you decided to undertake spiritual research into the caliber of your ancestors, you will never joke with marital battles. You do not need to delve too much into historical books before you will discover that our fore fathers had their baths in the pool of human blood. Some of our fore fathers pounded day old babies in the mortar for ritual purposes. Some of them were deeply involved in occult practices to obtain powers as warriors, warlords or tribal chiefs. They had to use dozens of human heads or bury pregnant woman alive.

In those days, toward off invasion from other tribes. Twin babies or albino were pounded alive. To be quite honest with you, a lot of unthinkable things were done. Unfortunately, modernity has not changed that spiritual status. What is more? Our ancestors were wicked. They actually dined with the devil. Some wicked ancestors were slave owners; others were so wicked that they perpetrated evil with reckless abandon. It is unfortunate that many are busy paying the debt owed by their grandfathers. No wonder the Bible says.

Ezekiel 18:19-20

Yet say ye, why? doth not the son bear the iniquity of the father? When the son hath done that which is lawful and right, and hath kept all my Statutes, and hath done them, he shall surely live. The soul that sinneth, it shall die. The son shall not bear the iniquity of the father, neither shall the father bear the iniquity of the son: the righteousness of the righteous shall be upon him, and the wickedness of the wicked shall be upon him.

THE MYSTERY OF YOUR ANCESTRY | 33

Long after the father have eaten sour grapes, the children teeth have been set on edge. This, indeed, is a great truth.

THE TRUTH ♦♦♦
The truth is the only weapon that can set you free. As the Bible has declared.

John 8:32
> *And ye shall know the truth, and the truth shall make you free.*

As far your marriage is concerned, only the truth shall set you free from the shackles of the marital problems which ancestral powers have set in motion.

> ***The truth is a powerful entity. Unless it is discovered and applied, you may continue to struggle under bondages. The truth will remain useless until it is known.***

It is of no value to the ignorant. The truth is very stubborn. Even if you try to subdue or kill it, it will remain strong. The fact that you have traveled far on the wrong road does not make it the right road. Again, it does not matter if there are many people going towards the wrong direction; once it is a road route then it's wrong indeed.

A wrong pathway will end up leading you astray. You need the naked truth if you must survive on the battle field of marriage. You shall know the truth. The truth you know shall set you free. The truth is that your marriage is of great interest to heaven. The other side of it is this; your marriage is also is of great interest to hell fire. God wants you to succeed. Satan wants you to fail. It is, indeed, strange that both heaven and hell are interested in your marriage. While heaven wants you to fulfill your marital destiny, hell wants the boat your marriage to sink. Beloved, heaven is waiting, hell is watching.

Here is another bitter truth. The enemy of our soul hates godly marriage with perfect hatred. The enemy can go any length to hinder you from discovering your divine partner in marriage. Even when you have discovered the right partner, the enemy can do anything in order to throw spanner into the works. It is unfortunate that a lot of marriages have been caged even when the partners were yet to be born. This has led to strange battle on the field of marriage. One terrible power that has caged a lot of marriage and enjoyed uncommon success is ancestral powers.

AN ANCIENT BATTLE ◆◆◆

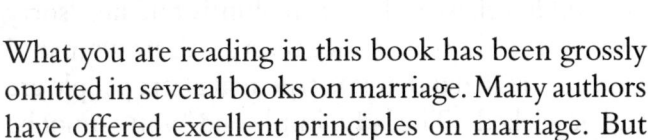

What you are reading in this book has been grossly omitted in several books on marriage. Many authors have offered excellent principles on marriage. But the missing ingredient is what we are examining in this book. Beloved, ancestral powers have pitched their tents and set battles in motion against marriages. You can hardly imagine that the type of battle people are facing are those started by their ancestors under the close monitoring of these ancestral powers. They have been in existence for so long and they have concluded the battle before you ever became aware of any spiritual scuffle going on. If you have listened to the kind of stories I listen to, you would have known that marital battle are legion. A lot of young men and woman have faced so much battle that they are no longer interested in marriage. Many have been dribbled and forced to shed tears. Many have contemplated suicide. Some have concluded that there is nothing like marriage in their dictionary.

A lady's first attempt at getting married failed mysteriously. This happen at the age of thirty seven; exactly a week to the wedding. The man started singing a different tune. He suddenly told her he was no longer interested in the marriage. The confused lady asked to know the reason behind the strange and sudden change. The man bluntly told her "sorry you are too short. I cannot marry a short woman. I have just realized that it is true that short people are bad or wicked". The lady simple said "you cannot be serious. Why did you not say this all through the period of our courtship? But, you knew that I was short when you proposed to me" the man replied with a blunt statement; "Please spare me all these semantics. I am not ready to marry you. Look somewhere else for your husband". He turned away without looking back. The lady suffered untold attacks. At age 39 another episode came up. It was tragic too. Exactly one week to her wedding, a driver suddenly lost control and ran the lady's would-be-husband to a wall. He died instantly and that was the end of the lady's second attempt at getting married. At that point, the lady ought to have known that something was wrong somewhere but she started looking for another partner. Ignorance had blinded her.

Beloved, ignorance is a disaster; it is the grandfather of misfortune. Every man's mountain is the mountain of his ignorance. The lady in question kept moving on blindly and at age 41, she managed to find another man. They both agreed and the wedding was fixed. In the lady's third episode, she actually went quite far in the journey. There was no tragedy prior to the day of wedding. Unfortunately, On her wedding day, disaster struck. As the marriage ceremony got under way, friends and families member became jubilant. The bride was dressed in a radiant white dress and she was beaming with smiles. The husband was also in high spirits.

But something strange happened. For those who have attended marriage ceremonies, there is a crucial aspect in the procedure of marriage which ministers quickly run through as they do not expect any negative occurrence. Here is the clause. "As you are seated here today to witness this holy matrimony, if there is any man or woman who has any reason or reasons why this man and this woman cannot be joined together in Holy wedlock let such a person speak now up now. Otherwise, let him or her be forever silent. Beloved, no gospel minister ever expects a negative response. But on that particular day the unexpected happened. While the congregation was waiting for the wedding service to be over, as soon as the pastor read out the popular clause, there was a strange noise at the rear end of the Church. A woman spoke in a feeble voice "I object". At that instance, cold sweat settled on the forehead of the officiating minister. It was impossible to go further. There was pin drop silence.

The pastor cleared his throat declared, "woman can you please come forward"? She sauntered to the front with a baby strapped to her back and another child was being dragged along. The officiating minister asked to know why she objected to the wedding being conducted. She made it very clear that she was legally married to the man. When asked to prove what had just declared, without wasting anytime, she brought out the marriage certificate. Some of the people that were at the wedding almost fell off their seats. Such a case had not come up in the history of the church.

The lady who was getting married was shocked to discover that she had taken another woman's husband to the altar. A man who was actually married with three kids was not her God-given husband. In fact, she fainted and had to be revived. That tragic experience drove her to the Mountain of Fire and Miracles Ministries. When she was brought to the General Overseer, God revealed to her the truth about her life. She was a victim of chronic marital ancestral problems, we discovered that she was the only lady in her lineage who attempted getting married, instead of giving birth to children as a single mother. It dawned on her that all the ladies in her family were busy producing children out of wedlock. She was the last of five sister and she decided to break the evil pattern. But she failed woefully. Obviously, she underestimated the facts that she with her siblings were under a serious ancestral yoke. The yoke was broken when she went through deliverance as a spiritual exercise where fervent prayers were said with determination and faith in the Lord Jesus, the truth deliverer.

Another incident took place in Abuja, the Federal Capital of Nigeria. A thirty nine year old lady attended one of our service. The Lord located her through a word of knowledge. In fact that was the final word of knowledge that day. Through the leading of the Holy Spirit, I declared "There is a woman here; a demonic serpent has been assigned against you. I have good news for you. That demonic serpent is dead. This is how you will know that this word of knowledge is meant for you. By the time you get back home, you will find a dead serpent in your apartment".

The lady in question could not imagine that the word of knowledge was meant for her.

However, she managed to say a dry amen, when I declared that the serpent was dead. She lived in a three story building and her flat was located in the topmost floor. Under normal circumstances, there is no way even a tiny snake could be found in such a high brow section of the city. The lady did not know that a surprise was waiting for her. By the time she got home, she had forgotten what I declared in the Church and she simply opened the door of her flat, switched on the light and entered her bedroom in order to pray. What she saw on the bed frightened her stiff.

Her first reaction was to run out of her flat. But, she suddenly remember that she was just coming from a prayer meeting conducted by Mountain of Fire and Miracles Ministries. Fear disappeared and faith took over. She boldly entered her bedroom in order to examine the strange object on her bed. Beloved, it was a huge python. The python's head was resting on her pillow. She tried to shake it off with every boldness she could muster. To her relief and surprise, the python was dead. The strange creature was so huge that the lady had to secure the assistance of hefty young men to drag the dead serpent out of her bedroom. That was how anti-marriage yoke was broken. The lady soon got married to a wonderful man. She later discovered that the python had hindered her from getting married for several years. If that yoke had not been broken, she would have remained single for life.

If you have studied history meticulously, you would have discovered that tragedy have been common features in the history of the family of the Kennedys in the United State of America. Many of them died mysteriously. Their history has been doted by series of series of tragedies. Although, they are affluent, popular and respected, ancestral powers have dealt seriously with them. Even the popular Wikipedia, the free online encyclopedia, records the death of the Kennedys as a 'family curse' and it further records 'The Kennedy tragedies, colloquially known as the Kennedy Curse.' The curse is applied to the family's nine children, thirty-one grandchildren, and sixty-five great-grandchildren and their spouses. It will sound ridiculous if after you go through the details of the Kennedy Tragedies and still decide to remain ignorant about ancestral powers. They were just victims of the Ancestral Powers we are talking about in this book.

Do you know that the royal family of England has also suffered mysterious attacks from ancestral powers? This shows that ancestral powers have no regard for royalty or wealth.

A lady in faraway Jamaica was secretly going through demonic attacks. Her situation was so strange that she had to go to her pastor to ask for spiritual help.

What was her problem? She had a permanent spiritual husband who was molesting her sexually. Either she was asleep or awake, an invisible being was having sex with her. Her story appeared too strange to her pastor and the pastor simply told her to seek psychiatric help. However, she knew that she was not suffering from any form of mental problems or attacks.

Out of desperation and frustration, she started searching the internet for help. Her search brought up the Mountain of Fire and Miracles Ministries. She personally bought her ticket and boarded a flight to Lagos, Nigeria. Without talking to anyone and getting any form of assistance, she found her way to the Prayer City of the Mountain of Fire and Miracles Ministries.

Her situation was desperate and she was bent on getting a drastic solution. While in Jamaica, she had exhausted every available option in order to solve her weird problem. While the deliverance session got under way, the deliverance minister came up with a prayer point that was strange to her; "Every spirit husband, harassing my life, die, in the name of Jesus". The concept of commanding a spirit to die appeared very strange to her. With a Master's degree in English and another degree in theology, she found fault with the prayer point. Her knowledge of stylistic and semantic weakened her resolved to pray.

She quickly came to grip with the fact that she had traveled a far distance in order to seek urgent help. She then decided to ignore all forms of rhetoric's and decided that whether she understood the prayer concept or not, she would pray anyhow. She suddenly became violent in her prayer. She was given a revelation instantly. The strange husband that had embarrassed her sexually every hour of the day and every day of the year appeared before her, visibly disturbed. The ground on which the spirit husband stood caved under him. That was how he sank into the ground and was buried instantly. At that moment, she obtained her deliverance. The strange sexual molestation that had lasted for twenty five years ended at the Prayer City. The lady has since been married. It took serious deliverance and prayer sessions for the lady to be set free from ancestral bondage. If she had not taken that step, she would have remained single till date.

CHAPTER TWO

Captives of the Terrible

Never underestimate the spiritual influence of your ancestors. The platform which your ancestors built before you were born is very strong. You must pray with violence if you want to become free and consequently pursue your marital dreams successfully.

3

CHAPTER THREE

3 Captives of the Terrible

The truth is that lots of ladies and gentlemen are victims of wicked ancestral powers. The bottom line is that ancestral powers have gone quite far in hindering men and women from getting married. Never underestimate the spiritual influence of your ancestors. The platform which your ancestors built before you were born is very strong. You must pray with violence if you want to become free and consequently pursue your marital dreams successfully.

Beloved, there is no denying fact that you are product of your ancestry. Most problems that people go through, in the area of marriage and destiny, are cause by ancestral powers. How then can we identify these ancestral power? What are the indications of the presence of the activities of the ancestral powers? How can you detect the fact that problems or delays in the area of marriage are occasioned by ancestral powers? The following are the things to look for.

ANCESTRAL POWERS ◆◆◆

1. **They are powers that are in charge of a family and rule wickedly from one generation to another.** The moment ancestral powers are involved, members of the family, in any generation, would go through terrible oppression, spiritual attacks, manipulation and violation. The right of family members would be denied them. In such families, marriages never work. There would be repeated occurrences or instances such as teenage pregnancy, single parenting etc. When ancestral powers are at work, the women always marry the wrong men while the men always marry women that will plan their pitfalls. In some families, high blood pressure would be rampant. In other families insanity or madness would be common occurrences.

When strange things happen in such families, no one would be able to give any clear explanation on the causes. When members of such families are sick, the best diagnostic machine would detect nothing.

2. **Power assigned to kill, to steal and to destroy.** Ancestral power always carry out missions of destruction. In such instances, it will be destruction galore, high mortality rate, virtues would be stolen and good things will suddenly vanish.

3. **Powers assigned to afflict a family.** Wherever such families are found, they would go through serious afflictions. Affliction manifests in various ways and it could be perpetual or intermittent. It could also be in form of a sickness that could be terminal or incurable. Apart from a careless lifestyle that could make someone contracts some diseases, ancestral power could also be the powers behind some family ailments.

4. **Ancestral powers can be described as powers that are assigned against a family.** It is possible for a strongman to be assigned

against certain area of someone's life. These include marriage, finance, career or health. When the strongman that is assigned is an anti-marriage strongman, getting married will be difficult; establishing a good home will almost be impossible.

5. **Ancestral powers are powers behind collective captivity.** Collective captivity describes the presence of an evil umbrella that keeps victims under bondage. The moment the mystery of collective captivity is in place, there will be strange occurrences in the lives of members of the family. The same evil trends would run through their live. Member of the family will continue to pass through the same circumstances, whether they are together or not. For example, if the assignment of the power of collective captivity happens to be lateness in marriage, everyone would get married late mysteriously. If the incident of collective captivity centers on having children out of wedlock, every effort towards getting married legitimately and raise stable families will be impossible. Collective captivity can be likened to an evil umbrella which shields all the

people under; away from the good things of life, including marriage.

6. **Ancestral powers are often assigned to discipline anybody in the family who is guilty of violating the covenants which their fore-father have entered into.** It is a fact that most of our ancestor, especially if you belong to the black race, were not serving God. They were chronic idol worshipers. The history of the black race was unfortunately entrenched in deep idolatry. Our fore-father entered into all sort of covenants. They performed all kinds of concoctions. Most families were covenanted and handed over to terrible idols. By the time you opt to come out of such a covenant, demonic powers shall rise up to mete out their own form of punishment to those who are guilt of desecrating or abandoning their altars. Ancestral powers generally fight back by mounting road blocks on the pathway of those who are undertaking journeys into marriage. These powers are extremely mean. They try to embarrass or cause problems for those who have abandoned idolatry, as a form of vengeance.

7. **Ancestral powers are the powers behind repeated evil family history.** When ancestral powers are angry, they trigger what can be referred to as an evil cycle. Some ugly incident will keep happening repeatedly. This incident will be visible in the lives of every member of the family. In some families, divorce is inevitable. In some other families, there will be breakdown of courtship or relationship. Members of such extended families often discover that no matter how hard they try, there would be repeats of dark occurrences in the family. Such occurrences are not normal. They are sponsored by diabolical powers.

8. **Ancestral powers often operate as blood line demons.** The blood is a very powerful entity. It functions as the life line that keeps human beings alive. There is so much power in the blood. This power is either used positively or negatively. Your connection with the blood of Jesus, for instance, will earn you positive benefits. On the other hand, any negative connection with the ancestral blood line can be used as a vehicle for conveying terrible attacks into the lives of victims. It has been said earlier that through the umbilical cord or the placenta,

every child is connected to the blood bank of his or her ancestry. Consequently, some wicked demons have decided to make use of the blood line to pass evil currents in form of attacks in the area of marriage. The activities of blood line demons are characterized by wickedness. Those who are attacked by these demons can be rightly described as "captives of the terrible".

9. **Ancestral powers are assigned to execute punishment of cursed families.** There is something called 'Generational Curse' which runs throughout a particular family for as long as the linage exists. Those curses were issued as a result of some incidents of the past. Most times, except by divine intervention, the incidents that led to the active curses are not traceably run effectively and without mercy. So it is these ancestral powers that monitor the continuity of the curses once a new baby is born into the family.

10. **Ancestral powers are the powers constituting the principalities in your heaven.**

Ephesians 6:12:
> *'For we wrestle not against flesh and blood, but against principalities, against powers, against the rulers of the darkness of this world, against spiritual wickedness in high place'.*

The principalities mentioned here are the ancestral power we are talking about. They block the heavens over their victims making a very simple thing very difficult.

11. **Ancestral powers are the evil powers genealogical assignment.** They are the powers that hold tight to the constant flow of certain features in the lineage of a family. that is, once you mention the names of those that made history in a particular family, certain features are dominant in their lives which mark all of them for who they lived for. These dominant feature such as 'gross anger' 'chronic pride,' etc. are actually negative and since they did not know Christ they glory in them.

12. **Ancestral powers are the spirits that are claiming to be spirits of the dead members of the family.** There some people

who are experts at summoning what they referred to as the spirit of the dead. They could call out such spirit to ask question over any cloudy things to them. This is a lie from the pit of hell: once a man dies, his spirit can no longer be called out for any earthly assignment again. The power behind this confusion are the ancestral powers. Since they practically know everyone in the family, including their secrets, they could act them when summoned. But once you are born-again and you have prayed yourself into total freedom from their grip, they find it impossible to act you.

13. **Ancestral powers are also called the hereditary powers.** They are the spirits that make the hereditary of negative traits, behavior or disease possible in a particular family line. They monitor such traits to make sure all their victims in the family possess and duly act them to their own detriment.

14. **They are the dark powers some people were born with.** Hope it's not new to you that some babies were actually born and they grew up behaving strange and abnormal. They were

possessed right before they were born and they act strangely, mysteriously and are source of pain and heartache to their parents. The evil spirit dictating their action are the ancestral powers. I pray that you shall not fall victim of such strange children, in the name of Jesus.

These are just some of the manifestation of ancestral powers. The mystery of the ancestral marital attacks is deep. Ancestral power are legal experts. They go to the roots of victims, plant evil seeds and watch painstakingly until it is time to afflict. Most of the activities of ancestral powers are carried out in the area of marriage. Since the major preoccupation of these powers is to make use of the strength of ancestry to establish their stronghold and carry put their wicked activities in any family that is formed in the lineage. They are very quick to establish their domination, manipulation and attacks in every potential family.

Immediately you begin to plan to set up your own family, they target the new home as a unit where their evil tentacles can be established. They make use of their primordial knowledge and hidden strength to affect anyone who happens to be an offspring. These power have done so much and are still planning to carry out their wicked plans in the future. Most of the time, acute health problem in the family, courtship failure, inability to find or locate a spouse, strange hindrances to marriage, being attracted to the wrong partners, sudden hatred for one's partner and unexplainable tragedies when men and women are almost concluding their marital plans and such unhealthy developments are strong indications that ancestral power are at work.

By the time you put a halt to the activities of ancestral powers in your destiny, life and marriage, negative indication will disappear and positive ones will become visible. By the time you remove their grip from your life, then ninety percent of your problems are over.

CHAPTER FOUR

Spiritual Diagnosis

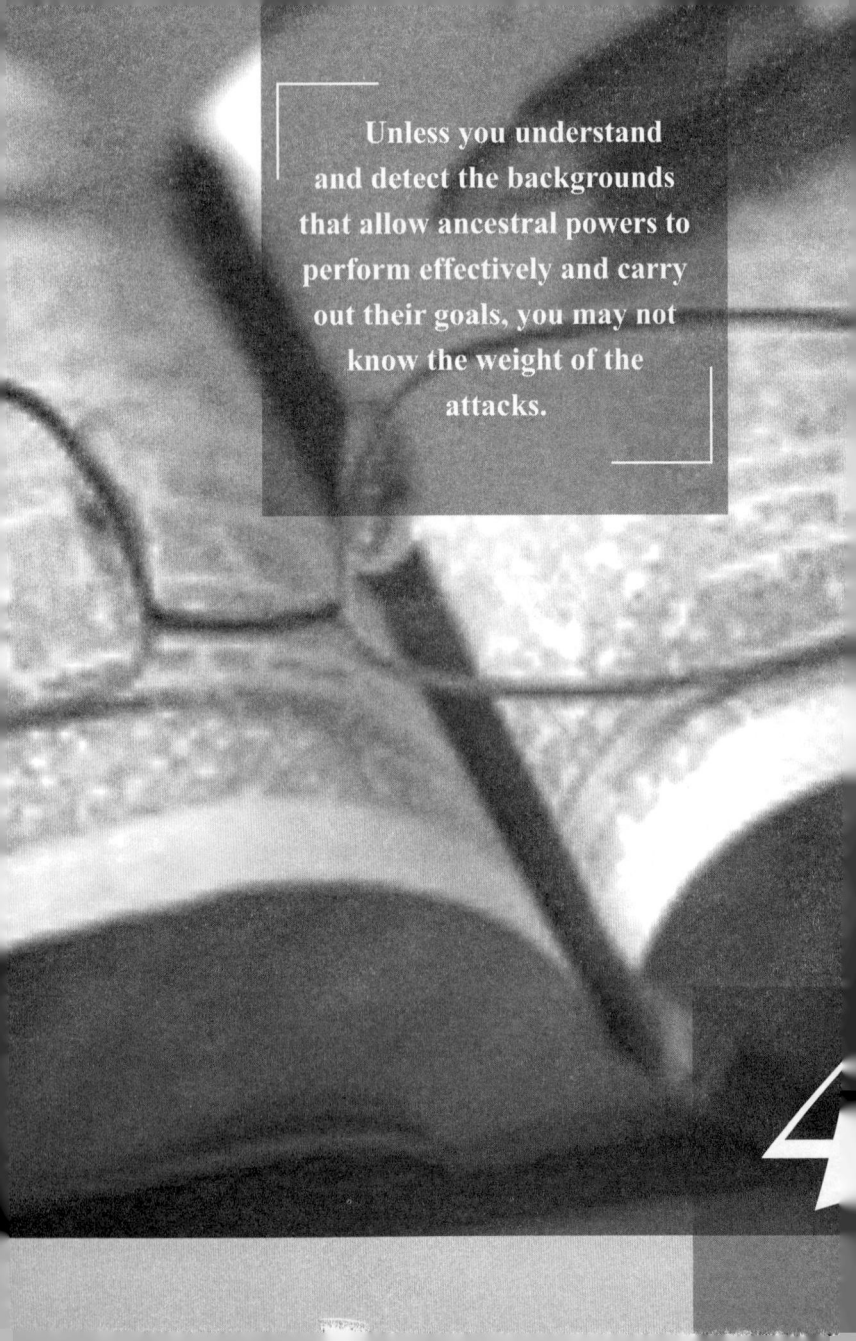

Unless you understand and detect the backgrounds that allow ancestral powers to perform effectively and carry out their goals, you may not know the weight of the attacks.

CHAPTER FOUR

SPIRITUAL DIAGNOSIS

Several years ago, I handled a strange case. The victim was attacked by ancestral power. A seventy year old man who had ministered for over fifty years was involved in a scandal. He was found in his office committing fornication with a twenty years old lady. He was suspended from the ministry and that was what brought him for deliverance. The ancestral power that pursued his family line also pursued and disgraced him because we discovered that it has been a trend in his family. During ministration, it was discovered that his polygamous foundation disgraced him in spite of the fact that he had spent over fifty years in the ministry. Ancestral powers can wait patiently for fifty or more years to disgrace or ridicule their victims. They can go very far and make unusual sacrifices in order to capture their victims. You need to pray aggressively in order to obtain freedom from them.

To deal with the ancestral powers that have been assigned to frustrate you in the area of marriage, you must understand the following facts. Unless you understand and detect the backgrounds that allow ancestral powers to perform effectively and carry out their goals, you may not know the weight of these attacks. Ancestral power do not operate in a vacuum. So, the moment the reasons are strong and the victim comes from a background that can be described as ancestral stronghold, there would be serious attacks at every stage of the marital journey.

Beloved, here are the reasons why lots of Bachelors and spinsters are finding it difficult to get married. Even for some that are married already, having a marital bliss is a no go area for them. To be quite honest with you, due to the ancestral foundation of some ladies and men, many may not get married at all, except serious deliverance prayers are put in place. The following facts must be considered if you want to successfully discover the reasons for repeated attacks in your marriage. If you have

SPIRITUAL DIAGNOSIS | **63**

discovered the following in your background after through research, then the hard battles you have fought, so far, in the area of marriage are not ordinary. If any of the factors listed below are found in your ancestry, then you have a lot of battle to fight and a lot of prayers to do.

THE BACKGROUNDS YOU MUST WATCH! ◆◆◆

1. **If you come from a background of idol worship, you will experience marital delay, disturbance and failure.** As long as there is any history of idolatry in your foundation, getting married will obviously be very tough. Here, there is need to pause and meditate. Several years ago, most communities in the third world were deeply entrenched in idol worships. Most communities and villages were doted by fetish altars. The atmosphere was so dark that thousands of idols were worshiped and several days were dedicated to idolatrous festivals. Although, the situation has changed, the fact that there has been an idolatrous past cannot be ignored. The idolatry which your ancestors got involved with is, without doubt, taking huge toll on certain

aspects of your life today. As long as you come from a background of idol worship, you will experience strong oppositions and attacks. There would be evil cries from the altars of your fore-father. Since most of the altars have become restless and are now fighting back. Since covenants were formed with ancestral idols, the powers of the idols will try to rear up their heads and come up with fresh demands. Failure to meet up with these demands would lead to problems and disturbances in marriage. Ancestral powers, when they feel neglected or challenged, they try to block your marriage, attract the wrong spouse and make you experience closed heavens over your marital life. These powers often shoot the arrows of neglect, hatred or spiritual evil covering. Consequently, the victim will suffer form what can be described as invisible syndrome. Ancestral powers will put a veil on the victim; the person will neither be noticed nor appreciated by the opposite sex. If you have come from this kind of background, you may discover that ladies and men that you are far better than maybe getting married with ease while, with all your degrees, good social status excellent disposition and good conduct, members of the opposite sex may act as if you do not exist at all. Those who come from places where idolatry is rampant generally go through battle, when they begin to contemplate marriage. Ancient idols are very jealous and stubborn. They hate to see children of those who worshipped them several years ago get married successfully. There would be frustration, confusion, spiritual manipulation and total breakdown and failure of marital plans.

2. **If your ancestors were members of the masquerade cult, you will experience instability in your relationship or marriage.** The spirit behind masquerades will trouble you seriously. Victims will experience stagnancy in their relationships and immorality will suddenly come up. The relationship will be veiled or covered spiritually. Partners or couples will be barred from seeing each other's good side. Those who have history of masquerades in their background will be so veiled or blinded that whatever will make their marriages glorious will remain hidden from them. Those who

grew up from the background of local masquerade festivals will be blindfolded when they want to know God's will in marriage. Such people often pray without receiving any revelation from the Lord concerning whom to marry. When people from such background are in courtship, there will be no form of transparency. If they succeed in getting married, such couple will cover a lot of things up; they will not be true to each other. There will be lying, exaggeration; deceit as the spirit of the masquerade would prevail over their lives. The severity of the attack often depends on the type of maquerade cult their ancestors were involved in. if your ancestors were devotees or very powerful and dangerous masquerades there would be terrible ancestral attacks. Unless ancestral yokes are broken and the powers of the masquerade are paralyzed, victims will continue to be mysteriously influenced through the remote control gadget of ancient masquerades.

3. **If you are from a polygamous home, your marital journey will face terrible stumbling blocks and your marriage will face strange attacks.** Those who come from

polygamous home often find it hard to keep a healthy relationship. Ladies from such background will experience multiple proposals that bring confusion and complex negative advances from men. Men from such background will suddenly discover that their marital journey is often embarrassingly complex. Sexual weakness will be a common trend. Ladies from polygamous homes generally lose their virginity at very tender ages. While others discover their God-given partners with ease, people from polygamous homes will experience multiple courtships that breaks up too soon as if they are in a sport. People from that kind of background often experience marital distress and general backwardness. If you probe people from this kind of background, they will confess that they have had multiple partners. As one partner is leaving, another one is just coming into the scene. Let me be very blunt here, anyone who comes from a polygamous background must, of necessity, go through deliverance. If your future is very important to you and you want to avoid problematic courtship and marital turbulence, ultimately, you must be free from all the problem that are attached to the polygamous foundation. If there is an evil flow of the spirit of polygamy into your life, you may end up with the effects of polygamy springing up here and there in your life. Are you reading this book as a married couple? You need to go back to your foundation and be set free from the spirit of polygamy that was attached to your placenta. However, I have good news for you. The power that sets free from ancestral bondage will set you free completely. Every spirit of polygamy programed into your life shall catch fire and release you, in the name of Jesus. The power of polygamy that caught up with your parents will not catch up with you, in the might name of Jesus.

4. **If you come from an ancestry of fetish priests, witch doctors and voodoo priests, there will be lots of problems in your marital experience.** Children of fetish priests and witch doctors often grow up to face serious setbacks in the area of marriage. The spirit of witchcraft and the power behind fetish practices will continue to trail people from that kind of backgrounds wherever they go.

Victims will experience what can be described as a stinking agenda. Unexplainable mysteries will dog the steps bachelors and spinsters from such a polluted background. They will experience marital pollution, confusion and manipulation. The steps that are taken to get married will not be straight forward. Ladies and men from the homes of witch doctor and fetish priests will be influenced by the spirit of evil divination. When such people pray to know the will of God in marriage, they might experience conflicting signals. Victims will experience strange hatred wherever they go. There will be constant failure and terrible spiritual attacks. When such people try to locate their spouses, they might come across those who are possessed with terrible kinds of spirits. The fetish practices of their ancestors will catch up with them even when they are ignorant of such an evil flow. Are you from such a background? Have you experienced mysterious or strange happenings in your marital life? You need to break evil covenants or jinxes that are troubling your life as a result of your ancestral past. The fact that your ancestors were involved in sorcery, divination and fetish practices should make you to easily detect the effects in several areas of your life, including marriage. You need deliverance, yoke breaking prayers and definite efforts to sever the rope that binds you with your ancestors in this area. If you are familiar with the extent to which witch doctors and fetish spirits go, you will no longer be surprised that people from such homes often suffer terrible setbacks in life. To obtain power, some witch doctors go too far. Some of them have pledged an embargo on every marriage in their lineage. Unknown to many who are living today, their marriages were used as collateral, several years ago, to obtain evil power from the devil's bank. To withdraw the collateral, serious prayers are needed. Many witch doctor have used the substance in the life of their offspring. These offspring now go about with empty shells. May God help those who fall into this category, in the might name of Jesus.

5. **Marine Worship:** This is another serious area. Those who come from a background of marine worship often face serious problem in their marriage. If your mother or grandmother was a marine priestess, you will surely experience hindrance in marriage. If you have

discovered that the worship of water spirit was prominent in your lineage, you cannot afford to fold your hands as if there is no problem. In some parts of Africa for example, some families are devotees of water goddesses like Olokun and Yemoja, most especially in some parts of Nigeria. When children from this family grow up, there will be slippery marital breakthroughs Mermaid spirits will erect strange stumbling blocks in order to frustrate the marital journeys of their victims. Ladies or men from this kind of family are often attached to wicked partners. Whether they are in courtship or married, their partners will continue to punish or maltreat them. Such people will experience marine attacks physically and spiritually. Those who come from this kind of background are often addicted to sex. The ladies will receive conflicting and embarrassing advances, she will offer herself to as many men as possible. Ladies with marine background are often possessed by the spirit of seduction. Such ladies are often raped and abused sexually wherever they go. Even when they are married, they go into extra marital affairs. Those who come from the background of marine worship are erratic in their behavior. They are unstable when they are proposed to. They are heartless when they relate with their spouses or partners. They are controlled from the water kingdom. The ladies have spirit husbands, the men have marine wives. Any home that is under the yoke of marine spirits will continue to experience strange problems, instability and financially insufficiency. The only solution here is deliverance by aggressive prayers. The captives of the terrible shall be delivered. People from marine background sometimes have to go through multiple deliverance sessions. The signs to watch for include strange breakup of courtship, lack of focus, the problem of indecision, wicked manipulation, inability to locate your divine partner, insensitivity to the needs of your partner and acting as if there is another relationship somewhere. Victim act and talk strangely. Scandals are common. Strange problem are normal occurrences. Victims of marine attacks experience sexual molestation in their dreams. Their sexual libido is unnatural. Such victims easily pick up quarrel with their partners. They go to extremes in their dressing patterns. When they are corrected, they flare up. They are not ready to come authority. Problems that are related to marine attacks can only be solved spiritually. Partners who patch up such problems will eventually experience monumental failure in marriage. Marine spirit are very wicked. When they begin their attacks, they hardly give up. The only solution is to break the power and the influence of the marine kingdom over your life

6. **Slave Trade:** The slave trade is not only an occurrence in history, it has great consequences. If your ancestors were involved in slave trade, do not be surprised if the opposite sex is using you as a toy. If you come from a lineage of slave dealers, your life will continue to attract those who want to exploit you. If nothing is done, the mystery of 'use and dump' may hit you like a canker worm. The type of partners such people will live like slaves, bringing in everything and receiving nothing in return. Whenever such people want to get married, their partners would die mysteriously. It will be clear that curses are working against the victim. Slaves were subjected to terrible conditions. The pain was huge. The maltreatment was monumental.

The wickedness experienced was monumental. The wickedness experienced by slaves was beyond what anyone could bear. Most of the slaves issused curses against the generations of those who sold them into slavery. People from certain cities that were notorious as centers for the illicit slave trade often experience terrible hindrance in marriage. The involvement of our forefathers in slave trade is affecting many people today. The spirit of slavery has captured many homes. Consequently, a lot of ladies and men keep meeting strange stumbling blocks each time they take steps towards getting married. There must be serious aggressive prayers, heartfelt confessions and deliverance before this problem can come to an end. Though the slaves are no longer alive but the curses spoken into the air are still damaging many lives today. This may be the reason why your marriage has remained under a siege. The earlier you deal with issues the better.

7. **Occultism:** If your parents were into the occult or they spent their lives consulting many fetish priests or witch doctor, you are

Spiritual Diagnosis | 75

likely to be affected by such an aged practices. If you grew up and noticed the presence of charms in your parent's house, if you noticed that there are strange incisions on your body, then you are a product of an occultic background. If your parents participated in occultic practices of various dimensions. The power behind such practices will definitely affect your life. The history of involvement in occultic practices might have fainted in your memory but occultic powers will never forget the pledges made by our forefathers. The invisible power of the occult will keep magnetizing, negative people to you. Victims will live under the yoke of profitless hard work. Tragedies will occur at random. Partners will be slippery and strange hands will continue to guide the affairs of the victims. The occultic practices which your forefathers got involved with will unleash negative problems on your life. If your forefathers acquired wealth illegally, through the power of the occult, this power will begin to siphon your wealth to their own bank if your forefather attained prominence through the power of the occult, you will notice that no one will notice you when you're in the crowd. This power will ensure that every benefits enjoyed by your ancestors would be converted to a deficit in your life. Serious prayers are needed here. If you want to possess your possession in the realm of marriage, there are more ancestral battles you must fight and win. So far, we have discovered that ancestral problems are affecting many people today.

8. **Stealing:** if your ancestors were involved in stealing, either minor or large scale, what they did might be affecting you today. Those who are raised from families where stealing was rampant will suffer the consequences, sooner or later. It is worse when your parents or ancestors were burglars or they aided thieves. Their past deeds will affect you. If you have noticed incurable diseases in your lineage, it is one of the consequences of the actions taken by your parents. Those who come from this background are often victims of stolen relationships. Their partners are stolen by their best friends or co-workers. In certain instances, when some people get married, their husband are snatched away from them. Ladies or men from these kind of families often experience lack of commitment from

SPIRITUAL DIAGNOSIS | **77**

their partners. Good things are often stolen from those who come from this background. A partner who has given his or her consent suddenly disappears and is nowhere to be found. When these kinds of things happen, you must undertake a thorough research into your background.

9. **Bastards:** This is another terrible problematic foundation. Children who are rejected by their fathers or those who were born in circumstance where no one can be pointed at as the real father often go through lots of problems in life. If your ancestors were bastards, you will notice strange problems in your life. Victims would live unprofitable lives; they generally lack vision. They are not ready to pursue any dream. Those who come from this kind of background face rejection mysteriously. When they are in a crowd, no one would want to come near them. There will be many things in the life of the victim that scares others away. If there are bastards in your family, strange problems will come up. Getting married will be difficult; making progress in your marital journey will be hard.

10. **Local Hunters:** some families in ancient times were hunters. They raised the entire family through hunting. In Africa, an average hunter will not just go into the forest to kill animals such as Lion, Elephant and other wild animals. Hunters often make use of powerful charms. Some forest in Africa were inhabited by strange spirits. No hunter could go into such terrible locations without making use of some fetish powers. What our forefathers went into could not have been ordinary. Such things have great consequences. If you come from a family of hunters, do not be surprised if you are struggling to make it in life. If your ancestors were hunters, strange problem will come up now and then in your life. You may find yourself been attached to the wrong partners. Your partner would always be overly protective. They will exhibit extreme jealousy. You will be highly emotional. You may often act as if you been pursued. You need deliverance if your parents were hunters. Left overs will be assigned to you. You may notice that you are not free to live a life that is completely free. Children of local hunters experience ugly attacks. There will be no freedom to pursue your dreams in the area of

marriage. Until children of hunters go through deliverance, it will be difficult to live a settled life. You need deliverance today.

11. **Drummers:** In some communities in Africa and in some parts of Asia, the act of drumming is a vocation or a commercial venture. Drummers perform in occasions or move from one place to another to drum as a means of entertainment. Consequently, they receive financial tokens or payment. Some aspects of drumming are still demonic till date. Drumming is an essential aspect during fetish occasions. Those who come from the ancestry of chronic drummers are plagued by the spirit of poverty. Lack of direction and over subscription. Those who have discovered the history of drumming in their ancestry often marry ladies or men who end up draining their finances. Drumming is such a mysterious practice; hence we do not allow it in the ministry. If you have detected lack of direction, confusion and excessive patronage, the spirit of the local drum is at work. In those days, local drummers get whatever they want from the people they entertained by making use of charmed drums. When they go for any outing

they are loaded with charms in order to subtly hypnotize those who patronize them. By the time they have carried out commercial drumming for a long time, they would have had fellowship with terrible demons. The far reaching effects of such local practices often affect their children. You need to cancel the effect of fetish drumming today.

12. **Royal Families:** Royalty is often respected. But, behind the glamour of royalty, there are deep foundation problems and battles. If you happen to come from a lineage of royalty then you are likely to live a life of an exotic fish swimming round in an aquarium or a monumental fish bowl. Such people live according to royal dictates; they are not able to live their own lives. Royal problems abound. Those who come from royal families are under influence of powerful royal spirits. When one of the partners is a member of a royal family, the other partner become a common peasant. Ladies or men who come from royal ancestry love giving orders. They are often domineering and love to be obeyed by everyone. They are self-opinionated, snobbish and somewhat proud. They are not ready to

humble themselves and get married to a partner that has been divinely chosen for them. Either during courtship or at the instance of the marriage ceremony, people from this background want to show off. They are addicted to a show-glass life style. If you come from a royal family, do not be surprised if you are over rated. Such people may appear too handsome or pretty. They may also have too much wealth to lavish but when the essence of true marriages is considered, they have nothing to offer. To be quite honest with you, ladies or men from royal families need deliverance from royal bondage; they must also be set free from the problem that royalty has imposed on them.

13. **Incest:** Incest is a descriptive term for strange sexual occurrence between two people who are blood relation like a father and daughter. In the past, there are instances of incest in some ancestry and this has led to instances of marital failure. When a father abuses his daughter sexually, the result will be felt by several generation. When such aberrations are in place, the spirit of hindrance will be at work. There will be loss of interest in relationships.

Incest has often resulted into hatred for marriage. Ladies who are victims of incest in their families or in their personal lives are not ready for any form of involvement in a marital relationship. They are often touchy and negative. Temper tantrums are common. Such ladies get angry easily. They also find it difficult to go along with others. They are moody and keep to themselves. They quarrel with colleagues and neighbors. The trauma that is associated with the strange problems called incest often makes victims to be disoriented. Beloved, there is another type of incest that is responsible for marital problems today, it is called spiritual incest. This occurs when someone sleeps with his or her pastor, counselor, deliverance minister, group leader or general overseer. Incest is committed when a pastor is sleeping with his or her children in the Lord.

14. **Trading in alcohol or tobacco.** When this is common in your ancestry, there would be lots of problems. If your parents or any of your ancestors were ever involved in alcohol or tobacco business, your life and marriage will be affected. Involvement in such a trade would

have spoilt people's lives. Children of such traders will also experience a lot of problems. If you are constantly harassed by spirit husbands or spirit wives, I challenge you to check your background. If you are always losing good relationships and opportunities, something is wrong somewhere. Men and ladies who are always making wrong choices are obviously paying the price of ancestry involvement in the sale of alcohol or tobacco. You need deliverance if your parents were into such trade or business.

15. **Town criers:** Town criers, in those days, were local palace assistants who helped the king to pass across useful information to the entire community. The local town crier, though faithful, often lived below the poverty level. Those who come from such families are affected by the spirit of town crier. By the time the town crier goes through the length and the breath of the community, he would have acquired enough demons to subject his lineage to backwardness, failure, restlessness and instability. Children from such families though attractive, would be troubled by the spirit of rejection. They generally experience

turbulent relationships, tragedies, mysterious occurrence and all kinds of problems. If you want to make progress in your marital plan, you need to purge your life from town crier's spirit.

16. **Concubine:** Concubine age is an extension of polygamy. Either children were produced or not, your ancestors had concubines. As a result of wealth and popularity, some of them had chains of secret lovers who either married or single. Some of them even eloped with other people's wives and were later cursed. Those who come from such families often enter into relationship with unfaithful partners, slippery lovers, and deceitful partners. They are involved with sugar coated ladies or men. Most of the time, they discover that other men or women are trying to get involved with the partner they have chosen to marriage. The spirit of the concubine will fight back sooner or later. It will constitute serious hindrances when important steps are being taken.

17. **Cultural Dancers:** Cultural dance forms an integral part of cultural festivals in communities. Though cultural dancers enjoy

being watched when they entertain during public functions but there is more to it than wriggling their bodies and performing all types of acrobatic displays. The dancers often receive dangerous spiritual arrows. If you come from a family of cultural dancers, you have a price to pay. Those who come from such families are attacked by the spirit of the vagabond. Consequently, they lack direction and vision. Such people are not serious. People do not take them serious as well. They are not able to keep and maintain a healthy relationship. Instead of being serious in life, they do things for show. The spirit of cultural dancing must be broken. To have a sold home and a good marriage, you must be free from the dancing spirit.

18. **Aggression to missionaries:** if you come from a lineage where there was aggression to missionaries who were spreading the gospel, you need to do a lot of confessions and prayers. Our forefather killed missionaries and were also resistant to the gospel. Many of our forefather fought against Christianity and disgraced servant of the living God. Hence, the dust of vengeance has continued to afflict the entire lineage. Great consequence are attached

to all forms of hostility and attacks against missionaries. No wonder, those who are from such families are grappling with general blockage and closed heavens. They are struggling under the cobweb spirit and spiritual doors for success already closed door against them, no matter where they are. Simple steps have become problematic. What could have been achieved with ease have been attempted several times without success. Unless there is total repentance and plead for mercy, there is no way people from such families can make appreciable progress.

19. **Human Ritual or sacrifices:** Our ancestors were involved in all types of sacrifices including human ritual. If your forefathers were engaged in human sacrifices, there will be untimely death in the family. Women will grow old and remain virgins. Those who come from families where rituals were carried out generally have their lives turned upside down and they experience horrible dreams and nightmares. They will discover that they are mysteriously restless. The effect of such rituals and sacrifices are often seen in many generations. Such people may see apparitions

SPIRITUAL DIAGNOSIS | **87**

and ghost. Victim must go through deliverance exercise.

20. **When parents were womanizers or flirts:** those whose ancestors were busy changing men or women at random will experience similar traits in their own life. Do not be surprised if you experience turbulence in your marriage. it is simply because what the ancestors did, has been recycled spiritually and passed into the lives of men and women in that family. Victims will suffer chronic diseases, recurrent tragedies and constant failure. People from such ancestral background often have unfriendly friends too.

21. **Those whose ancestors were involved in maltreating the Jews:** those who come from this kind of foundation often suffer serious affliction because the Jews were tagged to be God's own with a lot of covenant hanging on their existence. Even from history, all the people that have attempted to wipe them off from earth died mysteriously.

22. **Land Grabbers:** Our forefather stole lands and acquired lots of landed property from

people illegally, thereby depriving people of what belongs to them. Every land stolen or acquired forcefully has great consequences. The offspring of those who perpetrated such things often experience general backwardness in life, fail where others succeed and they become embarrassed when their partners are mysteriously stolen. Children of land thieves generally loose valuable things in life. You need to go through deliverance, if you come from these background.

23. **False prophets and religion:** There are false prophets and fake religions are found all over the world. Several year ago, there was lot of local white garment churches with lots of self-styled prophets. These fake prophetess did a lot damages in the lives of worshippers. If your parents or ancestors were fake prophets who made use of satanic divination to give false prophesy and pronouncement that ruined people lives, you must not be surprised if the same spirit of deception is working against your marriage. If you have been misled by negative prophesy and you are now having opposite dreams, the false prophesy of your ancestors have caught up with you. When you

mistakenly conclude that your enemies are your friends and your friends becomes your enemies, it is a symbol of ancestral pollution.

24. **If your parents were conscious or unconscious witches or wizards.** As long as there is witchcraft in your family line, the powers of foundational witchcraft will attack your marriage. Witches or wizards generally conscript succeeding generations into the witchcraft society. Victims will experience constant harassment by the powers of darkness. Such powers will block marital breakthrough and any form of progress in life. The life of the victim attracts polluted partners. Any trace of witchcraft in the family has automatically made you a candidate of urgent deliverance. If you happen to come from communities where children were named after witches or they are given names that celebrate the power of witchcraft, you must run to the deliverance ground as fast your legs can carry you.

25. **If your parents were highly fetish nothing will work for you.** In those days, there was serious competition among families in other to

prove that one family is more rooted in fetish practices. There is nothing to be proud about in been fetish. The more your parents were deeply involved in fetish or diabolical powers, the more you need to be pitied. The fetish activities of your parents will invite battles into your life. The partner such people will be attracted to will equally be fetish. Victims and their spouses will be involved in hypnotism and other forms of occult acts. Efforts will yield little or nothing. People from fetish background will find it difficult to live a successful Christian life.

26. **Murderers:** The human blood is a powerful entity. The moment it is shed, it will continue to fight. Children or offspring of murderers will face strange problem in life. Every blood shed by your ancestors will testify against you unless you go through genuine deliverance. You must raise up the blood of Jesus against any evil blood. The blood which your ancestors shed will appear and reappear to threaten your life. The only antidote is to have the blood of Jesus to speak mercy into your life.

27. **Sodomy:** These are homosexuality,

lesbianism, bisexualism, etc. if you come from these kind of foundation, there will a lot of sexual confusion, and the person will lose interest in the opposite side totally. If your parents practiced any form of perverted sexual acts, your marriage will be affect. You must drag the influence of your parents' sexual sins to Calvary. You need to pray and go for deliverance.

28. **Bad names**: Check your family names. Bad names make people to repeat errors and it will release evil patterns into a person marital life. There are some name you should not bear, no matter how stylishly the name is pronounced. Any family name that is joined to idols, that has to do with reincarnation must not be used. Demonic names must be changed. The effect of evil ancestral names must be cancelled before any tangible progress can be measured.

29. **Masturbation:** if there is any history of masturbation in your ancestral life, you need to pray. If you come from the foundation of masturbation, you may never be free from spirit wives and spirit husbands until you go through deliverance. The masturbation which

your ancestor's got involved with will make it difficult for you to pursue your personal marital program. The spirit of masturbation will repel your partner and you may not be able to enjoy your marriage.

30. **Divorcees and broken homes:** product of divorce and those who come from broken homes are generally affected in life. Such people may take every required steps and follow every laid down principle but they will still fine it hard to achieve success in marriage. The spirit behind divorce and broken home will work against them. People from this kind of experience generally go through broken relationship, broken engagement and inability to keep a stable relationship. Neither are they able to build a home.

These are some of the activities of wicked ancestral powers. In believe that you have discovered areas where you have been attacked.

CHAPTER FIVE

Steps To Freedom

Right from the beginning of every godly marriage, the kingdom of darkness often comes up with battles. As the journey progress, the battles increase.

CHAPTER FIVE

STEPS TO FREEDOM

At this point, you need to deal with and overcome ancestral powers. You must obtain freedom from the powers of your father's house. For your marriage to be wholesome there must be total freedom. Every evil pipe drawing ancestral problems into your marriage must be set on fire. You must counter the poison of ancestral power. To have a successful marriage and experience complete success, the following steps must be taken;

THE STEPS ◆◆◆

1. **The new birth:** you must be born again. Confess your sins and surrender your life to Jesus. The new birth takes you away from any

form of evil platform which was erected by your parents. As soon as you become born again, the devil has no legal power over you.

2. **Confession of sins:** You must confess every secret and open sins and ask for total forgiveness. Every unconfessed sin gives the devil an entry into your life. Strip yourself naked before the Lord and He will never neglect you.

3. **You must renounce all your sins:** Don't just confess your sins and asked for forgiveness, you must also make up your mind never to go back to them again.

4. **Prayerfully expose and destroy every form of evil foundation.** You may need to stand as an official representatives of your lineage by confessing ancestral sins and applying the blood of Jesus to the terrible platforms erected by your forefather.

5. **You need to repair the altar of prayer.** Demolish the altar of idolatry and build your life, destiny and marriage on a new altar.

6. **You need to build a new foundation by praying aggressively.** If your ancestors actually spent hundreds of years to put an evil foundation in place, to build a glorious foundation you must spend more than a few minute in prayer. The foundation will sustain you and shield you from attacks must be well built. Do not joke with this foundation since your life depend on it.

7. **You need to barricade yourself from any form of evil ancestral attack.** You need to put very strong spiritual immunity in place. You must not allow what is happening to others to happen to you.

8. **Finally, you need to examine yourself at this point.** In what area have you been affected by these powers? Have you experienced setbacks in your marital journey? Do you experience like father like son or like daughter like mother battle, or you have sex in dream? Any dream of dirty wedding gown? Any dream that you are married to a strange person in the dream. You find your shoes missing or stole in the dream (which represent marriage). Or you find yourself with only one pair of shoes in the

dream. Do you dream of having your hair shaven? Any dream about wedding day and no one attending the wedding? Do you eat in your dreams, or do you see masquerades in your dreams? Are you here, you find yourself returning to your old place like your primary, secondary school etc. you see yourself swimming in water? It means you have a war to wage against ancestral powers.

Many years back I was in New York for a crusade in a place called Brooklyn. A white lady came for counseling and I felt so sorry for her because she did not know the forces she was battling against. She noticed that her great great-grandmother, great grandmother, grandmother and mother died of breast cancer. When she noticed the trend she quickly went to her surgeon and asked him to remove her two breast, despite the fact that there was nothing wrong with them. When the cancer eventually came, there was no breast to attack, it went ahead to attack her liver and it was this incident that brought her for prayers. It was from my mouth that she was hearing about ancestral powers for the first time. If there is any power that takes a man from hero to zero that brings a man from grace to grass, it is these ancestral powers.

A very powerful church somewhere in Europe was going down, until it was almost becoming nothing. Than a poor driver took over the church and it was in his hand that the church received a population explosion and became a rich and famous church. All of a sudden again, the ancestral powers that determine the fate of the then poor bus driver struck. He started by trying to sleep with church girls and the girls went to report to the police, and had this pastor arrested and jailed. The ancestral powers took him back to his poverty and he went back to his poor bus-driving.

Ancestral power are things you should not allow in your destiny. Most of our ancestors did not serve the living God, they served the devil and made alliances and entered into covenants with him. That is why the war against these powers should not be joked with. These forces may be in a family line for thousands of years and they might have defeated your parents and grandparents. By this, there will an urgent need for you to start a serious deliverance prayer to break free from these heartless demons.

There was a family in which no one lived above the age of 40. By the time they are getting to the age of 39 they would have a dream in which they would seven people carrying a coffin. That automatically meant that person was the next on line to die. Whenever that person who was usually the head of the family died, a new head of the family would be chosen. Then it came to the turn of a particular man who had been made head of the family and he was of the age of thirty nine and a half years old. He told his wife about the issues and as advised by some friends they ran to prayer city for deliverance. It was the deliverance program that the revelation of their foundation was exposed. They had a very powerful ancestor in their family line who was a king. When this king died, they buried seven slaves alive with him. These slaves issued a curse on that family that no one would grow above the age of forty. These slaves were the ancestral powers that were in charge of the situation of every member of their family. The curse they issued grew up to be ancestral powers that monitored the death of everyone who approached the age 40. What a wicked spirit!

Ancestral battles are real. When you make use of the prayer points at the end of this book you will experience unprecedented breakthroughs in your marriage, in Jesus' name. The powers that will not let you go will do series of spiritual somersaults and die.

You will be free to pursue your marital goals. Your steps will be smooth. You will find the right partner. Your home shall be built and your marriage shall be glorious. To be quiet honest with you, you have a lot of prayer battles to do. The results of the prayer session will depend on the aggression you put into every prayer point.

Prayer Section

1. Begin to confess your sins and those sins your ancestors committed.

2. Cover yourself with the blood of Jesus and envelope yourself with the fire of the Holy Ghost.

3. Sing this song-there is power, wonder working power in the blood of the lamb.

4. O Lord, empower my prayer altar by fire, in the name of Jesus.

5. O Lord, soak me in the spirit of prayer, in the name of Jesus.

6. Let God arise in Hid anger and fight for me, in name of Jesus.

PRAYER SECTION | **103**

7. I refuse to allow my angels of blessings to depart, in Jesus' name.

8. I paralyze all aggression addressed at my star, in Jesus' name.

9. Lord, bring honey out of the rock for me, in the name of Jesus.

10. Lord, open up all good doors of my life that household wickedness has shut, in the name of Jesus.

11. Let all anti-breakthrough walls design against my life be shattered to irreparable pieces, in the name of Jesus.

12. I paralyze all satanic antagonism from the womb, in Jesus' name.

13. I command open disgrace on the mask of the enemy, in Jesus' name.

14. I paralyze all evil legs rooming about for my sake, in Jesus name.

15. Let all evil blood that has mingled with my blood be drained out, in the name of Jesus.

16. I trample upon every enemy of my advancement and promotion, in the name of Jesus.

17. I break every evil collective unity organized against me, in the name of Jesus.

18. Let the backborn of the stubborn pursuer and strongman break, in the name of Jesus.

19. I destabilize the controller of any land of bondage in my life, in the name of Jesus.

20. O lord, enlarge my coasts beyond my wildest dream, in the name of Jesus.

21. Holy Ghost, seal all pockets that have demonic holes, in the Jesus' name.

22. Let the fire of disgrace fall upon demonic prophets assigned against my life, in the name of Jesus.

23. No dark meeting held on my behalf shall prosper, in Jesus' name.

24. I claim back my goods presently residing in wrong hands, in the name of Jesus.

25. Let the blood and strength of stubborn oppressors dry up, in the name of Jesus.

26. Let the head of every serpent power fashioned against me be broken, in the name of Jesus.

27. Throughout the days of my life, I will be in the right place at the right time, in the name of Jesus.

28. Powers that defeated my parents and are now fighting me, die, in the name of Jesus.

29. Ancestral marital blockage, die, in the name of Jesus.

30. Every arrow fired against my marital life, backfire, in the name of Jesus.

31. Powers of my father's house, release my marriage, in the name of Jesus.

32. Anti-marriage serpent and scorpions get out of my leg, in the name of Jesus.

33. Powers attacking my marriage shoes die, in the name of Jesus.

34. Ancestral powers, stealing my wedding garment and shoes, die in the name of Jesus.

35. Every familiar spirit initiation in my life, break in the name of Jesus.

36. Let the yoke of marital disappointment planted in my life scatter, in the name of Jesus.

37. Failure at the edge of my marital breakthrough I cut off from you, in the name of Jesus.

38. I pronounce this day that my marital life is not a specimen for satanic agents, in the name of Jesus.

39. Every witchcraft laboratory, experimenting on my marital breakthrough, catch fire instantly, in the name of Jesus.

40. O thou lying spirit, countering me before my God-given spouse, die, in the name of Jesus.

41. Any evil family carry-over in my life, blocking my marital joy, be cut off by fire, in the name of Jesus.

42. I decree that my marriage is not for sale, in the name of Jesus.

43. Whatever I need to change in my life in order for me to get married, Holy Ghost, help me to change them, in the name of Jesus.

44. Every character disorder, causing disappointment for me in life, receive divine touch of transformation, in the name of Jesus.

45. Every bad character, making me to be constantly disappointed in my marital destiny, receive divine touch for a change, in the name of Jesus.

46. I refuse to be married to the family idols of my father's house, in the name of Jesus.

47. I refuse to be married to the family idols of my mother's house, in the name of Jesus.

48. Embargo of marital disappointment, in my life break, in the of Jesus

49. I decree that enough is enough for jilt in my life, in the name of Jesus.

50. The last jilt I experienced shall be the last one forever, in my life, in the name of Jesus.

51. I receive the fresh oil to marry and stay married, in the name of Jesus.

52. Henceforth, let no man trouble my emotions for I bear in my body the marks of the marks of the Lord Jesus, in the name of Jesus.

53. Make this confession as you hold up your right Shoe in your hand. My father, I use this shoe as a point of contact to my marriage, any power working against my marital breakthrough is dead now in the name of Jesus. Let your fire fall upon my spiritual shoes. Any power that has stolen my marital shoes return them now by fire in the name of Jesus. I use this shoe as a point of contact for my marriage, oh God of the suddenlies; arise, arise, araise and plead my marital cause.

With the shoe now in your hand quietly tell the Lord when and where you want your marriage to be.

BOOKS FOR SINGLES BY DR. D. K. OLUKOYA

1) Choosing your life partner
2) Breaking the yoke of marital delay
3) 34 laws of courtship
4) Dominion prayers for singles
5) principle of Magnetizing Your Divine Spouse
6) 40 marriages That must Not Hold
7) Dating plus
8) 100 reasons why sex must wait until marriage
9) Fifty Reasons Why People Marry Wrongly

OTHER BOOK BY DR. D.DK OLUKOYA

1. 20 Marching Orders to Fulfill Your Destiny
2. 30 Things the Anointing Can Do For You
3. 30 Poverty Destroying Keys
4. 30 Prophetic Arrows From Heaven
5. A-Z of Complete Deliverance
6. Abraham's Children in Bondage
7. Basic Prayer Patterns
8. Be prepared
9. Bewitchment Must die
10. Biblical Principles of Dream Interpretation
11. Biblical Principles of Long Life
12. Born Great, But Tied Down

13. Breaking Bad Habits
14. Breakthrough Prayer For Business Professionals
15. Bringing Down The Power of God
16. Brokenness
17. Can God Trust You?
18. Can God?
19. Command The Morning
20. Connecting The God of Breakthroughs
21. Consecration Commitment & Loyalty
22. Contending For The Kingdom
23. Criminals In The House Of God
24. Dancer At The Gate of Death
25. Dealing With The Evil Power Of Your Father's House
26. Dealing With Tropical Demons
27. Dealing With Local Satanic Technology
28. Dealing with Witchcraft Barbers
29. Dealing With Unprofitable Roots
30. Dealing With Hidden Curses
31. Dealing With Destiny Vultures
32. Dealing With Satanic Exchange
33. Dealing With Destiny Thieves
34. Deliverance Of The Head
35. Deliverance of The Tongue
36. Deliverance: God's Medicine Bottle
37. Deliverance from Evil Load

OTHER BOOKS BY DR. D. K. OLUKOYA

38. Deliverance From Spirit Husband And Spirit Wife
39. Deliverance From Limiting Powers
40. Deliverance From Evil Foundation
41. Deliverance of The Brain
42. Deliverance Of The Conscience
43. Deliverance By Fire
44. Destiny Clinic
45. Destroying Satanic Masks
46. Disgracing Soul Hunters
47. Divine Yellow Card
48. Divine Prescription For Your Total Immunity
49. Divine Military Training
50. Dominion Prosperity
51. Drawers of Power From The Heavenliest
52. Evil Appetite
53. Evil Umbrella
54. Facing Both Ways
55. Failure In The School Of Prayer
56. Fire For Life's Journey
57. Fire for Spiritual Battles for The 21st Century Army
58. For We Wrestle
59. Freedom Indeed
60. Fresh Fire (Bilingual book in French)
61. God's Key To A happy Home
62. Healing Through Prayers

63. Holiness Unto The Lord
64. Holy Fever
65. Holy Cry
66. Hour Of Decision
67. How To Obtain Personal Deliverance
68. How To Pray When Surrounded By The Enemies
69. I Am Moving Forward
70. Idols Of The Heart
71. Igniting Your Inner Fire
72. Igniting Your Inner Fire
73. Is This What they died For
74. Kill Your Goliath By Fire
75. Killing The Serpent of Frustration
76. Let God Answer By Fire
77. Let Fire Fall
78. Limiting God
79. Looking Unto Jesus
80. Lord, Behold Threatening
81. Madness Of The Heart
82. Making Your Way Through The Traffic Jam of Life
83. Meat For Champions
84. Medicine For Winners
85. My Burden For The Church
86. Open Heavens Through Holy Disturbance
87. Overpowering Witchcraft

88. Passing Through The Valley of The Shadow of Death
89. Paralyzing The Riders And The Horse
90. Personal Spiritual Check-Up
91. Possessing The Tongue of Fire
92. Power To Recover Your Birthright
93. Power Against Captivity
94. Power Against Coffin Spirits
95. Power Against Unclean Spirit
96. Power Against The Mystery of Wickedness
97. Power Against Destiny Quenchers
98. Power Against Dream Criminals
99. Power Against Local Wickedness
100. Power Against Marine Spirit
101. Power Against Spiritual Terrorists
102. Power To Recover Your Lost Glory
103. Power To Disgrace The Oppressors
104. Power Must Change Hands
105. Power Must Change Hands (Prayer Point from 1995-2010)
106. Power To Shut Satanic Doors
107. Power Against The Mystery of Wickedness
108. Power of Brokenness
109. Pray Your Way To Breakthroughs
110. Prayer To Make You Fulfill Your Divine Destiny
111. Prayer Strategies For Spinsters And Bachelors

112. Prayer Warfare Against 70 Mad Spirits
113. Prayer is The Battle
114. Prayer To Kill Enchantment
115. Prayer Rain
116. Prayers To Destroy Disease And Infirmities
117. Prayers For Open Heavens
118. Prayers To Move From Minimum To Maximum
119. Praying Against Foundational Poverty
120. Praying Against The Spirit of The Valley
121. Praying In The Storm
122. Praying To Dismantle Witchcraft
123. Praying To Destroy Satanic Roadblocks
124. Principles Of Conclusive Prayers
125. Principles Of Prayer
126. Raiding The House Of The Strongman
127. Release From Destructive Covenants
128. Revoking Evil Decrees
129. Safeguarding Your Home
130. Satanic Diversion of the Black Race
131. Secrets of Spiritual Growth & Maturity
132. Self-Made Problems (Bilingual book in French)
133. Seventy Rules of Spiritual Warfare
134. Seventy Sermons To Preach To Your Destiny
135. Silencing The Birds Of Darkness
136. Slave Masters

OTHER BOOKS BY DR. D. K. OLUKOYA | **115**

137. Slaves Who Love Their Chains
138. Smite The Enemy And He Will Flee
139. Speaking Destruction Unto The Dark Rivers
140. Spiritual Education
141. Spiritual Growth And Maturity
142. Spiritual Warfare And They Stop You
143. Stop Them Before They Stop You
144. Strategic Praying
145. Strategy Of Warfare Praying
146. Students In The School Of Fear
147. Symptoms Pf Witchcraft Attack
148. Taking The Battle To The Enemy's Gate
149. The Amazing Power of Faith.
150. The God of Daniel (Bilingual book in French)
151. The God of Elijah (Bilingual book in French)
152. The Vagabond Spirit
153. The Unlimited God
154. The Wealth Transfer Agenda
155. The Way Of Divine Encounter
156. The Unconquerable Power
157. The Baptism of Fire
158. The Battle Against The Spirit Of Impossibility
159. The Chain Breaker
160. The Dining Table Of Darkness
161. The Enemy Has Done This

116 | YOUR MARRIAGE AND YOUR ANCESTRY

162. The Evil Cry Of Your Family Idol
163. The Fire Of Revival
164. The School of Tribulation
165. The Gateway To Spiritual Power
166. The Great Deliverance
167. The Internal Stumbling Block
168. The Lord Is A Man Of War
169. The Mystery Of Mobile Curses
170. The Mystery Of The Mobile Temple
171. The Prayer Eagle
172. The University of Champions
173. The Power if Aggressive Prayer Warrior
174. The Power of Priority
175. The Tongue Trap
176. The Terrible Agenda
177. The Scale of The Almighty
178. The Hidden Viper
179. The Star In Your Sky
180. The star hunters
181. The Spirit Of The Crab
182. The Snake In The Power House
183. The Slow Learners
184. The University of Champions
185. The Skeleton in Your Grandfather's Cupboard
186. The Serpentine Enemies

187. The Secrets Of Greatness
188. The Season Of Life
189. The Pursuit Of Success
190. Tied Down In The Spirit
191. Too Hot To Spirit
192. Turnaround Breakthrough
193. Unprofitable Foundations
194. Victory Over Your Greatest Enemies
195. Victory Over Satanic Dreams
196. Violent Prayers Against Stubborn Situation
197. War At The Market Square of Life
198. Wasted At The Market Square of Life
199. Wasting The Wasters
200. Wealth Must Change Hands
201. What You Must Know About The House Fellowship
202. When the Battle is from Home
203. When You Need A Change
204. When The Deliverer Need Deliverance
205. When Things Get Hard
206. When You Are Knocked Down
207. When You Are Under Attack
208. When The Enemy Hides
209. When God Is Silent
210. Where Is Your Faith
211. While Men Slept

212. Woman! Thou Art Loosed
213. Why Problems Come Back
214. Your Battle And Your Strategy
215. Your Mouth And Your Deliverance
216. Your Mouth and Your Warfare

YORUBA PUBLICATIONS
1. Adura Agbayora
2. Adura Ti Nsi Oke Ni dii
3. Ojo Adura

FRENCH PUBLICATIONS
1. Pluie De Priere
2. Spirit De Vagabondage
3. En Finir Avec Les Forces Malefiques De La Maison De Ton Pere
4. Que I envoutement Perisse
5. Frappez l' adversaire Et II Fuira
6. Comment Recevior La Deliverance Du Mari Et De La Femme De Nuit
7. Comment se Delivrer Soi-meme
8. Pouvior Contre Les Terrorites Spirituels
9. Priere De Percees Pour Les Hommes D'affairs
10. Prier Jusqu'a Remporter La Victoire
11. Prieres Violentes Pour Humilier Les Problemes Opiniatres

OTHER BOOKS BY DR. D. K. OLUKOYA | **119**

12. Priere Pour Detruire Les Maladies Et Les Infirmites
13. Le Combat Spirituel Personnel
14. Bilan Spirituel Personnel
15. Victorires Sur Les Reves Sataniques
16. Prieres De Combat Contre 70 Esprits Dechaines
17. La Deviation Satanique De La Race Noire
18. Ton Combat Et Ta Strategie
19. Votre Fondement Et Votre Destin
20. Revoquer Les Decrets Malefiques
21. Cantique Des Contiques
22. Le Mauvais Cri Des Idoles
23. Quand Les Choses Deviennent Difficiles
24. Les Strategies De Prieres Pour Les Celibataires
25. Se Liberer Des Alliance Malefiques
26. Demanetler La Sorcellerie
27. La Deliverance Le Flacon De Medicament De Dieu
28. La Deliverance Da La Tete
29. Commander Le Matin
30. Ne Grand Mais Lie
31. Pouvoir Contre Les Demons Tropicaux
32. Le Programme De Tranfert Des Richesse
33. Les Erudiants A l'ecole De La Peur
34. L'etoils Dans Votre Ciel
35. Les Saisons De La Vie
36. Femme Tu Ese Liberee

ANNUAL 70 DAYS PRAYER AND FASTING PUBLICATION

1. Prayer That Bring Miracles
2. Let God Answer By Fire
3. Prayer To Mount With Wings As Eagles
4. Prayer That Bring Explosive Increase
5. Prayers For Open Heavens
6. Prayers To make You Fulfil Your Divine Destiny
7. Prayers To make God Answer And Fight By Fire
8. Prayers That Brings Unchallengeable Victory And Breakthrough Rainfall Bombardment
9. Prayers That Brings Dominion Prosperity and Uncommon Success
10. That Brings Power And Over Flowing Progress
11. Prayers That Bring Laughter And Enlargement Breakthroughs
12. Prayers That Brings Uncommon Favor and Breakthroughs
13. Prayers That Bring Unprecedented Greatness & Unmatchable Increase
14. Prayers That Bring Awesome Testimonies And Turn Around Breakthroughs.